M000014447

DIARY
OF A
MINECRAFT
POLAR BEAR

BOOKS KID

TABLE OF CONTENTS

Day 1

I raced along the ground, loving the feeling of the ice crunching beneath my paws.

"Hey, Ferdinand!" called my friend, Quillion. "Do you fancy coming fishing one last time before we head home? A bunch of us polar bears are heading down to the creek."

"Oh – yes please!" I yelled back. "I can't wait to see the look on Rose's face when I bring back a huge mountain of fish." I changed direction and ran after the other polar bear to where other bears were at the water, delicious, juicy fish just waiting for us to catch them.

That's right. I'm a polar bear and I live in the ice plains with my friends and family. It's the best life in the world.

Right now, I'm off on a mission to bring back lots of fish to the other polar bears back home. Yes, there's plenty of fish in the lake near my shelter, but there's something about the fish that live in the creek a few miles north from where we live that tastes extra sweet and ever since my cub, Quinn, came along, I've always wanted to make sure that my family gets the very best food possible.

I came to stand next to Quillion, who was patiently crouching on the shore, watching the water for a sign of movement. Suddenly, quick as a flash, his paw darted out and he scooped up a squirming fish, adding it to the growing pile behind him.

"That was a good one," I complimented. "But I think I can get an even bigger one."

I gazed at the water, looking out for the telltale signs of a large fish. When they've survived long enough to get big, fish learn a lot of tricks to avoid polar bears, but no matter how clever they think they are, I can always outwit them. No fish can escape me!

"There!"

I saw the briefest of change in the outline of a shadow, but it was enough to reveal the hiding place of a huge fish and when I'd grabbed him, even I was amazed by just how large it was.

"Catch any more like that and we won't be able to carry them all home," joked Quillion.

"You're only saying that because you don't think you can do better," I countered.

"Oh really? Well if that's a dare, you're on!"

Quillion and I spent the rest of the day competing with each other to see who could catch the biggest fish. He managed to get some real monsters, but none of them were quite as big as the first one I'd caught.

I really am the best fisher-bear in the tribe.

Day 2

We'd finally finished with our fishing expedition and packed up the fish to carry them home. I couldn't wait to get back to my wife, Rose, and our cub, Quinn. I've missed them so much. Quinn is the cutest little bear you ever did see, with a darling button nose and eyes so dark they're almost black, as well as soft, soft fur of the purest white. It makes him very difficult to see against the snow and ice, but that's the point. Nobody will be able to steal him away from us because they'd never be able to find him to take him.

Now you might be asking yourself who'd be foolish enough to steal a polar bear cub in the first place? After all, they'd have to face the wrath of an angry mama bear and a fearsome fully grown pack leader, but humans are peculiar creatures who seem to think that they can do whatever they want. I've heard plenty of stories of Minecraftians snatching polar bear cubs just because they thought they'd make good pets.

Ridiculous when you think about it. A fully grown polar bear isn't just enormous. We eat a lot of fish every day. And I mean a *lot* of fish. Why would you want a pet that was bigger than you who would eat you out of house and home? Surely the fact that polar bears are the most beautiful creatures in Minecraftia isn't a good enough reason to bother?

I guess I'll never understand humans.

The thought of my wife and cub made me run even faster. Although I'd only been away for a few days, it was the first time I'd left Rose alone with Quinn and I'd missed them more than I'd have thought possible. As soon as I got back, I was going to sweep them up into the biggest bear hug the world had ever seen.

Day 3

At last, I spotted the edge of our territory on the horizon. It wasn't going to be long before we were back home and I couldn't wait to see Rose's face when she saw all the fish I'd brought back for her and Quinn.

I picked up the pace and it wasn't long before I could see Rose rushing out to meet me. The grin that spread across my face almost made me drop the fish in my mouth. I was back with my family!

"Ferdinand! Ferdinand! Thank goodness you're home," she sobbed, burying her head in my fur.

"What's wrong, Rose?"

"It's Quinn! Someone's taken him!"

The blood in my veins turned to ice, my stomach churned into knots as I asked her to repeat what she'd just said.

"Quinn is gone! I woke up this morning and went to give him his breakfast, but he wasn't in his bed and although

I've asked everyone, nobody has seen him. He's been cubnapped!"

"Raaaaar!" I saw red as I roared, enraged. Polar bears are usually believers in live and let live. We're generally peaceful creatures that don't bother the humans around us as long as they leave us alone, but now that someone's taken my cub, I'm angrier than I've ever been in my life.

Someone was going to pay for this.

"Don't worry, Rose," I soothed, trying not to let her see how worried I was. "I'll find our boy. If he disappeared this morning, then he can't have gone far. He's probably just being silly, playing hide and seek because he knows that daddy is coming home and he wants to play a game with me. Let's look around for him. He's bound to be around here somewhere."

"All right," sniffed Rose, but despite both of us spending the whole day looking for our son, he was nowhere to be seen. He wasn't in his favorite hiding places and he hadn't built a new snow den.

He'd vanished into thin air.

Day 4

I'd hunted until the sun went down and the zombies came out, but there was no sign of Quinn.

At sunrise, my mind was made up. I was going to have leave our home and track down the people who'd snatched him. There was no way he would have run away on his own like this. Someone must have taken him.

"Where was Quinn last seen?" I asked Rose, who had been up all night with me.

"Over here."

She led me to a clearing where the cubs all liked to play together. I started sniffing around, but it was difficult to find a trace of Quinn among all the other youngling scents.

At last, I caught a trace of my boy.

"He went in that direction," I announced firmly.

"So what are we waiting for?" said Rose. "Let's go after him."

"No." I held out a paw to stop her. "I need you to stay home where it's safe."

"Safe?" Rose laughed bitterly. "How can it be safe here? Someone stole my boy!"

"Even so," I insisted. "There are other polar bears here to protect you and you know that I run faster than you. I can travel faster if I'm on my own."

A tear trickled down Rose's snout, making my heart melt.

"Besides," I continued softly. "I need you to stay here in case Quinn comes home. How would he feel if he got back and thought his parents had abandoned him? There's still a chance that he's just playing a game and got a little lost. He might find his way back and you need to be here for him. Can you do that for Quinn?"

"All right," sniffed Rose, brushing away another tear. "Do you really think that he'll come back?"

"Of course," I smiled, but inside, I knew that there was no chance of Quinn returning unless I went to fetch him. Someone had snatched him and I wasn't going to rest until I'd rescued my cub. "Now you stay here and start preparing the fish. When I bring Quinn back, he's going to be starving and you know how much a growing cub can eat. Just make sure you save some for me, OK?"

"OK," nodded Rose.

I dropped a quick kiss on her snout and turned to run in the direction of Quinn's scent. Whoever the humans were who'd snatched him, they'd soon come to regret it. I was one angry polar bear and there was nothing more dangerous than a polar bear whose son had been stolen.

Day 5

I kept my nose to the ground, making good time as I retraced Quinn's steps. At this rate, I'd have him back with his mom by the end of the day.

However, when I crossed over a ridge, what greeted me on the other side made my heart sink. A fast flowing river!

I went down to the water, but whoever had taken Quinn had had the sense to take him across the water. I went up and down the opposite bank, but it was no good. I'd lost his scent.

All wasn't lost, though. I might not be able to smell Quinn, but there was something else in the air.

The aroma of wood smoke!

There was a human camp nearby and there was no doubt in my mind that they must be the ones who'd stolen Quinn.

Growling, I rushed off in the direction of the camp and I burst through the hedges to find myself right in the middle of a group of humans cooking a meal over the fire, acting as if they didn't have a care in the world.

Well, I was about to change that for them. Rearing up, I attacked the nearest human, knocking him out with a single, powerful blow. The rest of them scrabbled for their weapons, but I was too fast and too strong.

Snarling and roaring, I lashed out in all directions and I didn't even feel it when one of the Minecraftians managed to strike me with his sword, the attack making me even more enraged and lending me greater strength.

When I was finished, the humans lay all around the camp. Out of the corner of my eye, I saw another Minecraftian running off into the distance, but I decided to let him go rather than chase after him. I'd wiped out the camp and now it was time to fetch my boy.

"Quinn! Where are you, Quinn?" I called. "It's me! It's dad! You're safe now! You can come out."

I called and called until my voice went hoarse, but there was no reply, and despite tearing down the entire camp, there was no sign of my cub.

I was forced to face reality. The escaping human must have taken Quinn with him. Well, he was going to regret that decision. If he'd left him behind for me, then I'd have let him go free. Instead, I wasn't going to rest until I'd found him.

He wasn't going to escape a second time.

Day 6

After the battle, I needed to take some time to recover before going after the human. I found some fish at the bottom of a bag and I chomped it down. It tasted all right, but I'll never understand why humans insist on burning all their food. What's wrong with a nice, raw fish?

I took the briefest of naps, filled with nightmares of Quinn running away from humans chasing him, leashes in their hand to enslave him, and I woke up shouting his name.

I couldn't leave him in the hands of the Minecraftians. Who knew what those monsters were doing to him?

I got my nose to the ground to find the trail of the escaped human. With no sign of Quinn and still no scent to show me where he was, the Minecraftian was the only lead I had.

At last, I caught a whiff of the human's disgusting scent and I headed off after him. Although he might have a lead of a few hours on me, I would catch up to him in no time. Polar bears are so much faster than humans.

He couldn't evade me for long.

Day 7

I had blisters on my paws from running for days, but I didn't care. I had the human in my sights and he was going to give me back my son.

He'd built another camp right by the lake and I could see him up ahead, sitting in front of a fire. There was no sign of Quinn, but that just meant that he'd hidden him somewhere nearby, hoping that he'd fool me into thinking that he wasn't the one who'd stolen Quinn.

He couldn't fool me!

"Raaar!" I snarled as I bounded into the camp, but this time, instead of being unprepared, he rolled away from my attack, snatching up the sword that he'd left lying on the ground next to him.

"What are you doing?" he cried, swinging his sword at me.

"Getting my boy back," I cried, batting the sword away. Usually, the strength of my blows could make a human's arm numb, but he was braced for my attack and he spun round with his sword, cutting at my leg.

"Aargh!" A red slash opened up, the blood bright against my fur. The sight of it only made me more determined to attack the human and I jumped forward, intending to bite him. Once a polar bear has a human in their jaws, they never let go.

However, the human deftly dodged me and jabbed at me with his sword again. I leapt back just in time…

…but landed in the fire! My fur caught fire and I was forced to run into the nearby lake to put out the flames.

"Why are you fighting me?" the human shouted at me.

"You know why!" I roared.

"I really don't," replied the human. "We were just minding our own business when you attacked our camp. I thought polar bears left humans alone unless we hurt you first."

"You *did* hurt me first!" I yelled. "You stole my cub!"

"Your cub?" The human's forehead wrinkled in confusion. "I have no idea what you're talking about."

"Yes, you do," I insisted, wading out of the water now that the flames were doused. "And you're going to tell me where he is or I'll beat the information out of you."

I raised a paw menacingly.

"Whoa!" The human backed up, holding his hands out in a peace sign. "I'm telling the truth. I haven't seen your cub. I wish I had. I promise you that if I'd seen him, I'd tell you where he was, but I haven't heard anyone talk about a polar bear cub."

I shoved my face up close to his, examining his expression for any indication that he was lying, but at last I was forced to concede that he was telling the truth. Probably.

"Quinn!" I wailed, slumping to the floor. It was all too much. After days chasing him with little food or sleep, exhaustion overwhelmed me. It was hopeless.

"Hey, big fella." The human patted me comfortingly on the shoulder. "I'm sure you'll find him. Where did you last see him?"

"That's just it," I moaned. "I left him and Rose behind while I went on a fishing trip. It was so stupid of me. If I'd stayed home with them, Quinn would still be safe."

"Don't blame yourself like this," said the human. "You didn't know. You were only doing your best to provide for your family." He thought for a moment. "Tell you what. Why don't I help you find your cub? I can talk to the Minecraftians for you. They might tell me things they wouldn't tell you. You can be quite scary, you know."

"I know," I sighed. The human's idea made sense, but it felt strange agreeing to work with one of them. Everyone knew that Minecraftians were untrustworthy. But what choice did I have?

"All right," I nodded at last. "You can help me. I guess I need all the support I can get right now."

Day 8

Heinrich – for that was the human's name – and I were sitting by a camp fire, toasting fish. Well, to be accurate, Heinrich was toasting fish. I was munching down some raw fish before he could spoil them by cooking.

"So tell me more about your cub," said Heinrich. "What does he look like?"

"He's adorable," I beamed. "His fur is all soft and fuzzy and he has the biggest, dark brown eyes."

"Does he have any distinguishing features, anything that makes him look different to the other cubs?"

I scrunched my face up as I thought. What a strange question! Polar bear cubs were all unique. Why wouldn't he be able to see that?

"He's my Quinn." I shrugged my shoulders.

"OK. Tell me all about what happened when you discovered that he was missing."

I told him all about the events of the past few days, starting with the fishing trip and ending up with how I'd destroyed his camp, thinking that he and his friends had concealed Quinn somewhere around.

"I'm really sorry for hurting your friends," I told him.

"They weren't my friends." Heinrich waved away my apology. "Truth be told, I didn't really like them all that much. They were talking about finding a mine and killing all the spiders living inside. I don't understand why anyone would do that. Spiders don't hurt anyone. They're our friends!"

I wasn't so sure about that. Their large, hairy legs gave me the creeps. Still, if this human didn't like the thought of hurting animals, then he really wouldn't have had anything to do with cubnapping Quinn.

"Anyway, I was planning on leaving them behind," Heinrich went on. "I'm an explorer, not a fighter. I've been making a map of Minecraftia. I hope that one day people will use my maps to plan out trade routes, bringing them closer together instead of fighting all the time. Here. This is what I've done so far."

He pulled out a piece of paper from his backpack and spread it out across the floor. I crowded around, curious about his work, but the squiggles he'd written across the page made no sense to me.

"Maybe we could use this to help find Quinn?" suggested Heinrich. "There are a few spots nearby that would be good places to camp. Perhaps his cubnappers are using one of them?"

"Good idea," I nodded. "Let's start at the closest place and work our way round. Wherever they are, they can't be far."

Day 9

"There. Just as I thought."

Heinrich beamed and pointed to a camp by the lake. It was further south than where I'd found him, but I could see why the Minecraftians had stopped there to rest. There were trees to provide some shelter and it was near a river, so there was plenty of fresh water and fish to be had. It was a good place to camp.

It was also a good place for me to ambush.

"I'm coming to get you, Quinn!" I yelled, running forward to attack.

"No, Ferdinand. Come back!" Heinrich called after me, but it was too late. These were the vagabonds who'd stolen my cub and I wasn't going to let anything get in my way, not even a human with a map.

I barged into the camp, sending equipment flying and knocking over shelters as I called for Quinn. He had to be here somewhere!

"Quinn! Quinn! Where are you?" I cried desperately, but there was no reply.

"Help!"

A human crawled out from underneath a shelter I'd destroyed and raced towards the lake to get away from me, but there was no escaping my wrath.

Have you ever seen a polar bear swim? We're fast, I tell you! If the human thought that he could swim away from me, he was about to be sadly mistaken.

I dove into the water, my legs working furiously to catch up with the Minecraftian. It wasn't long before I was able to reach out and grab him with my paw.

"Where's my cub?" I ducked the human under the water and let him back up again. "Where is he?"

"I don't know what you're talking about," the human spluttered, coughing up water.

"Ferdinand! Stop!" I turned to see Heinrich waving frantically at me from the shore as I prepared to dunk him again. "Quinn isn't here."

"If he's not there, then where is he?" I let go of the human in my confusion. He started swimming again, but I wasn't going to let him escape. Just because he didn't have Quinn in his camp didn't mean that he didn't have valuable information.

I made my way back to shore, dragging the man behind me. If he knew anything about Quinn's whereabouts, anything at all, he was going to tell me if he knew what was good for him.

Day 10

"Aa-choo!"

The human huddled by the fire Heinrich had built, sniffing and snuffling. I didn't have any sympathy for him. If he hadn't gone into the lake to get away from me, he wouldn't have caught a cold and anyway, I was sure that he knew something about what had happened to Quinn.

"Here you go." Heinrich handed him some soup and the human accepted it gratefully.

"Do you have to be so nice to him?" I complained.

"Yes, I do," replied Heinrich patiently. "If you want people to help you, they're far more likely to give you what you want if you're nice to them." He turned to the human. "Now, what's your name?"

"Ashley."

"Hi, Ashley. I'm Heinrich and this is Ferdinand."

I rolled my eyes. Did we really have to go through all of this?

Heinrich noticed my impatience, but ignored it. "Ferdinand has lost his cub," he explained. "He was wondering if you knew anything about what might have happened to him."

"A polar bear cub you say?" Ashley sat up excitedly. "Yes, I have seen one."

"You have?" I couldn't believe my ears. "Where? Where is he? Tell me!"

"He would if you let him get a word in," commented Heinrich dryly.

"I saw a cub on a leash in a camp not far from here," Ashley said. "It's just up river."

"That's it. We have to leave right now."

I got up to go, but Ashley put out a hand to stop me.

"Wait," he cautioned. "Don't go running into their camp without being prepared. There are a lot of Minecraftians there, experienced warriors who won't be easy to fight. They won't be frightened of you, the way-"

"The way you were?" I finished.

Ashley blushed and nodded.

"Thank you, Ashley," said Heinrich. "We really appreciate your help. Do you want to camp with us overnight?"

Ashley looked at me, clearly worried that I was going to attack him in his sleep. "Thanks for the offer, but I think I need to move on."

"To warn your friends who stole my son?" I growled.

"On second thoughts, I think I will spend the night with you," gulped Ashley.

"That's more like it," I nodded.

Day 11

I could barely sleep that night knowing that Quinn was so near and yet so far. Heinrich had spent the previous evening talking to Ashley, trying to get as much information from him as he possibly could. I could understand that it made sense to plan our attack if these were seasoned fighters, but I was desperate to rescue my son. Every minute I waited was a minute longer for poor old Rose worrying at home about her baby.

I needed to reunite my family as quickly as possible.

As soon as the sun rose, I insisted that we pack up camp and hit the road. Ashley ran off in the opposite direction of us, wanting to get as far away from me as he could. I didn't blame him. He'd seen how frightening a polar bear could be and that was nothing compared to what I was going to be like once we found the other camp.

"Wait! Don't you want to have some breakfast?" asked Heinrich, hurriedly packing up the last of his things and running after me as I loped down the trail in the direction of the other camp.

"No time," I called back after my shoulder as I picked up my speed. "I need to get my boy!"

I didn't care whether Heinrich stayed with me or not. All I wanted to do was find the camp. As the day wore on, it became harder and harder to run, but I pushed through the pain. I was going to rescue Quinn.

"Ferdinand!" Heinrich panted. "You must stop to rest, have something to eat. If you don't, you'll run out of energy and you'll never be able to save Quinn."

"Nothing will stop me saving Quinn!" I raged, but it wasn't long before I had to admit that he was right when I was forced to take a break. I simply couldn't keep running.

Heinrich built a small fire and started to heat up some food while I ate some of the fish he'd brought for me. As soon as I'd wolfed it down, I stood up, jogging from paw to paw as I waited for Heinrich to finish his meal. The second he'd finished chewing, I was off again.

Quinn was near. I could feel it in my bones.

Day 12

As we continued to race towards the place where Quinn was being held, the landscape gradually changed, the ice plains becoming increasingly dotted with trees and bushes. It became harder and harder to keep up my fast pace as I had to maneuver through the undergrowth, but I pushed on, ignoring the pain when I bumped into a branch or tripped over a root.

"Oof!"

What was that? Trees don't talk!

THUNK!

An arrow flew threw the air and buried itself deep into the trunk of a tree next to me.

"Skeleton attack!" shouted Heinrich, pulling out his sword. "You just ran over his foot!"

"I'm sorry – I didn't mean to." I panted an apology, not wanting to waste a second longer than necessary but it wasn't enough for the skeleton.

"For such an insult, you must die!" it screamed, launching into attack.

I dodged left and right, narrowly avoiding the arrows until I was within paw reach of the skeleton. Although they do a good job of trying to scare people, they're nothing more than a bunch of bones and no trouble for a big polar bear like me.

"You should have left it alone!" I roared at the skeleton, raining down blows. All my frustration at having my son taken away from me came pouring out and the skeleton didn't stand a chance.

"That'll teach you not to mess with a polar bear," I sniffed at the pile of bones in front of me. "Heinrich, come on. Let's get out of here. Heinrich? Heinrich?"

I turned and saw my friend slumped against the base of a tree.

"Heinrich!" I rushed over to his side. "What happened?"

"One of the skeleton's arrows hit me," he groaned. "I'll be all right, but I'm going to have to rest for a while. If you could build a fire for me that would be a huge help."

I bit my lip in indecision. I really needed to catch up with the humans who had Quinn, but it was my fault Heinrich had been injured. I couldn't just leave him here like that.

"All right," I said at last. "I'll get some wood."

Day 13

I spent the night with Heinrich to make sure that he was OK, but by the next morning, he still wasn't ready to move on.

"I'm sorry, Ferdinand. My leg is really sore. I won't be able to walk on it. But I know the area we're going to really well. Even if the people who have Quinn pack up the camp, I'll be able to track them down without any problems, I promise."

I shook my head. "I can't take that risk," I told him sadly. "This is the closest I've been to Quinn for days. If he disappears now, I don't know if I'll ever be able to find him again. I hate to say it, Heinrich, but I'm going to have to leave you here. Thanks for all your help so far, but I'm going to have to go after my son. I'll leave you enough wood to keep the fire going for today but after that, you're on your own."

"You can't just leave me like this," pleaded Heinrich as I started to gather up more branches and sticks to keep him warm in the ice plains. "I'll be all on my own and I can't walk properly. What am I going to do if more skeletons come along?"

"There won't be any more skeletons," I reassured him. "We don't get many around here anyway, but if you did see one, just wave a thigh bone at them." I passed him one of the bones left behind when I'd taken out the skeleton the day before. "They'll see it and know that you're a mean, skeleton killing machine, so they will leave you alone."

"What if the bone just makes them really angry?" countered Heinrich. They might go nuts and tear me limb from limb!"

"Now you're just being silly," I scoffed. "Skeletons are cowards. It's why they use a bow and arrow. That way they don't have to get close enough to their victims to risk being hurt. I promise you that you're in no danger from skeletons. If you're worried, then sit here until I come back with Quinn. You can come back to my home and stay with the other polar bears for as long as you like, I promise."

"But... but..."

I turned and ran away. I couldn't listen to Heinrich's protests any more. As much as I was grateful to him for all his help, I still needed to get my cub and bring him home.

Day 14

As I ran down the path, I couldn't get Heinrich out of my mind. I was haunted by the thought of him sitting by that fire, alone and forlorn. Although I'd made sure that he had plenty to eat and drink, lots of firewood, and his sword within easy reach, that didn't change the fact that his leg was injured and he wouldn't be able to move until it had healed.

What if he was right? What if the skeletons did come back? He wouldn't be able to defend himself.

Sighing, I stopped running and turned back to go the way I'd come. I couldn't just abandon him like that, even if it meant that I'd have to wait another day before being reunited with Quinn.

As I headed back towards the place where I'd left Heinrich, I heard a sound that chilled me to the core.

GROAN!

"Zombies!" I gasped, picking up speed. Heinrich was right to be worried. I never should have left him alone.

"Don't be scared, Heinrich! I'm coming to save you!"

I burst into the clearing and saw Heinrich surrounded by zombies closing in, reaching out to take his brains.

"Oh no you don't!" I yelled, rearing up on my back legs and mauling the nearest zombie with my front paws.

Zombies are slow moving and stupid. The latter is why they try to eat brains. They think it will make them more intelligent. I'd never seen anything to suggest that their theory was right, but there was nothing they could do about the fact that they moved more slowly than a snail when it's trying to avoid going to the dentist.

It wasn't long before I'd defeated the zombies. The few who'd managed to avoid my paws disappeared off into the trees, looking for an easier target.

"Are you all right, Heinrich?" I asked anxiously. "You didn't get bitten, did you?"

"No," he replied, patting himself down. "Thanks to you, I'm safe."

"Well don't worry," I told him. "I'm not going anywhere now. I'm going to stay right here until you're ready to hit the road with me. Nothing is going to hurt you while I'm around."

Day 15

"All right, Heinrich," I said the next morning. "Are you ready to hit the road again?"

"Sure."

Heinrich tried to pull himself up to his feet, but as he tried to put weight on his injured leg, he cried out and sank back to the floor again.

"I'm sorry," he wept. "I'm more badly injured than I realized. I can't go anywhere until my leg heals. You go on. You've already saved me from the zombies. I'll figure out a way to stay safe until I can catch up with you. Go get your cub."

"No." I shook my head. "I can't do that. What kind of polar bear would I be if I left you here, knowing that the zombies have already tried to ambush you once? If I wasn't here, you'd be zombie dinner. No, I'm going to stay by your side until you're ready to move on. I'll build a shelter for you to keep you comfortable. You get some rest and focus on healing."

"Thanks, Ferdinand," whispered Heinrich, closing his eyes.

I'd never built a shelter, but I'd seen humans do it plenty of times and if they could do it, then it couldn't be that hard.

Rearing up, I beat away at a tree, gathering wood to turn into planks. That's where I hit my first problem. My paws weren't very good at smoothing out wood and I ended up with splinters instead of planks.

"Fine," I muttered to myself. "If I can't make planks, then I can at least pile stones on top of each other and build a stone shelter that way."

I started gathering stones and piling them around Heinrich, but I struggled to get them to stay in place and when one particularly large boulder rolled towards the sleeping human, barely missing his uninjured leg, I had to admit defeat. If the stone had crushed his one good leg, he'd never be able to walk again.

I decided to stop wasting energy trying to build shelters. This was why polar bears didn't build things. Our paws were much better suited to fishing.

Instead, I started to patrol the clearing, walking round Heinrich in a circle, going counterclockwise then clockwise to stop myself getting bored. While I was here, no monsters were going to get anywhere near my friend.

Day 16

"So tell me more about yourself," I asked Heinrich. If we were going to be stuck here for a while, I figured that I might as well get to know my human companion a bit better. It was better than gnawing my nails away worrying about Quinn. "Have you been on lots of adventures?"

"Have I?" Heinrich shifted to get a little more comfortable. "I could tell you stories to make your fur curl!"

"Really?" My ears pricked up with interest. "Like what?"

"Well, there was the time I went to The End and ended up going to a pop concert by Endermen."

"Endermen?" I chuckled uncertainly. "Are you sure? I mean, they weren't just humans dressed up as Endermen? I didn't think that Endermen had even heard of music, let alone made it."

"Oh yes," nodded Heinrich. "They do. It turns out that Endermen are big fans of rock and pop and four of them got together to form the first Endermen band. The songs were really rather catchy."

He hummed a few bars of a tune, snapping his fingers in time to the music, but it didn't sound like anything out of the ordinary to me.

"But if you went to The End, how did you get out?" I asked. "I thought it was impossible to leave unless the Ender Dragon opened up a portal for you or you defeat her and forgive me for being rude, but I can't imagine her doing anything for a human nor you being strong enough to defeat her."

"I'm not," confirmed Heinrich. "Instead, I hid near her nest, watching her movements and seeing how she spent her days. Every now and then, a creature from The End would persuade her to open up a portal for them. I considered disguising myself as an Enderman and seeing if she would do the same for me, but it turned out that I didn't have to. She opened one up for an Endermite and I was able to follow it out, squeezing through the portal before it closed."

"Really?" I tried hard to contain my disbelief, but I guess it was a more plausible explanation than the notion that someone who'd been so easily harmed by a skeleton could defeat a dragon.

"Yep. Then I found myself in a castle. A really big castle. A *giant's* castle!"

"Giants? I didn't think they existed."

"Oh yes, they exists all right," nodded Heinrich. "And there's a castle to prove it. It was one of the scariest places I've ever been. Everything was so big that there was nowhere for me to hide. I had to run around the edge of enormous rooms, hoping that the giant wouldn't come in because I'd be spotted immediately. Fortunately for me, it was the middle of the night, so the giant was asleep, snoring so loudly that the walls of the castle vibrated at the sound! I managed to sneak out and run away but then I ended up in a swamp."

"A swamp?"

"A horrible place," Heinrich told me, his nose wrinkling at the memory. "It stinks of stagnant water and it's impossible to make it through without your feet getting soaking wet. After what seemed like hours of struggling through the swamp I saw a little hut, so I decided to take shelter in it, only to discover that a witch lived there. She was *not* happy when she found me asleep in her bed."

"I can imagine," I murmured. "What happened next?"

"She pulled out a splash potion and threw it at me, screeching at me to get out. It narrowly missed me, exploding against the wall, the wood steaming where the poison hit it. I pulled out my sword and tried to defend myself but witches are surprisingly good at fighting and in The End, I had to give up trying to hurt her and instead pushed past her and out to the swamp, running away as fast as my legs would carry me."

I yawned and settled my head between my paws as Heinrich continued to regale me with stories of the things he claimed to have done over the years. For someone who couldn't even get out of the way of a skeleton's arrow and barely managed to avoid becoming zombie dinner, he seemed to have been in an awful lot of life threatening situations and survived to tell the tale. I was beginning to wonder just how much of what Heinrich was telling me was true and how much of it was his vivid imagination.

I snickered as I imagined what really might have happened. When he saw the Ender Dragon he probably pooped his pants and she opened up a portal for him just to get rid of the smell! I doubted that it was a giant's castle. I bet it belonged to a normal person, who gave Heinrich a change of clothes before sending him out into the world again and as for the witch, well, everyone knew what witch's huts looked like. If Heinrich had been stupid enough to think he could take shelter in one, no wonder he'd been attacked. However, I thought it more likely that he'd seen the hut and ran away from it screaming.

Next he'd be telling me that he'd just happened to grab handfuls of potion on his way out…

"Luckily, I managed to snatch up a couple of potions as I left," Heinrich finished.

I couldn't help it. I burst out laughing.

"What's so funny?" Heinrich's forehead wrinkled in confusion.

"Oh, I'm sorry," I said. "I thought you'd made a joke. I must have misheard you."

"I've still got the potions in my bag," Heinrich told me, pulling out a couple of bottles from his backpack. "I figured that we could use them against the people who've cubnapped Quinn."

I felt awful. I'd been making fun of Heinrich in my thoughts while he was thinking about how we could rescue my son.

"Thank you, Heinrich," I said at last. "With any luck we won't need them, but it's good to know you've got them, just in case."

Day 17

Heinrich stood up, cautiously moving around the clearing as he tested his leg to see if it would bear his weight.

"It's a lot better," he finally announced. "I think I can walk on it. You'll have to help me, though."

"Not a problem."

Heinrich put a hand out to grab a handful of fur on my back and we set off, but progress was painfully slow in every sense of the word.

"I'm sorry, Ferdinand," Heinrich apologized. "I'm holding you back. I feel terrible about this. If only there was a way I could move as fast as you."

I thought for a moment and then slapped my forehead with my paw.

"Of course!" I exclaimed. "Why didn't I think of this sooner? Do you think you could climb on my back?"

A look of understanding spread across Heinrich's face as he nodded. I knelt down to make it easier for him to get up and after a few failed attempts accompanied by groans and winces, the human was finally sitting on my back.

"Get a tight hold of my fur," I instructed. "I'm going to run as fast as I can and I don't want to think about how much it'll hurt if you fall off at that speed."

"Don't you worry about me," replied Heinrich, using his knees to grip my back tightly. "I'm not going anywhere – except to rescue Quinn."

"Let's get going, then."

I roared with excitement and started to run as fast as I could. It felt good to finally hit the road and despite all the delays, I knew that we were going to catch up with Quinn soon. I could feel it in my bones.

Day 18

We spent as little time resting overnight as possible. With Heinrich on my back, I was able to make up a lot of lost ground and not long after the sun rose, I sensed something that gave me the first sign of hope we were drawing near to our target ever since Quinn had first disappeared.

I smelled him in the air!

"Heinrich!" I gasped. "Can you smell that?"

Heinrich took a deep breath. "Sorry, Ferdinand. I can't smell anything. The cold has blocked up my nose."

"You'll just have to trust me when I say that Quinn is over there, then."

"Quinn is in that direction?"

I could feel Heinrich sit up straight as he tried to catch a glimpse of the camp where my cub was being held.

"I can't see anything," he finally said.

"That's because we're still a few miles away," I told him. "But my nose is never wrong and I can smell my prey from even greater distances. I promise you, Quinn is being held somewhere over there. We should be able to see the camp tomorrow and then I'm getting my son back, no matter what it takes."

Knowing how close we were gave me a boost of energy and I started running faster than I ever had in my life, Heinrich almost falling off my back as I lurched into action. I didn't care though. Nothing was going to keep me away from my son now.

Day 19

We crested a ridge and at last, we saw a camp up ahead.

"That's it!" I whooped. "That's where Quinn is. Brace yourself, Heinrich. I'm going to burst into the camp and the safest place for you is on my back so you don't accidentally get hurt. Have those potions at the ready. Throw them at anyone who looks like they're going to attack us."

"Wait!" Heinrich cried sharply as I was about to pounce into action.

"What now? The camp is just there. I need to get Quinn back."

"I know, but I think you should take some time first to scout things out. Remember what that other human said? There are a lot of people here and they're highly trained warriors. Do you want Quinn to witness his father being slaughtered?"

"No," I sighed, although I couldn't imagine any of the humans getting close enough to me once I was on a rampage.

"Right. So let's just take our time to spy on them and formulate a plan that's going to work. The most important thing is to get Quinn out of the camp without him getting hurt, isn't it?"

"It is."

"So let's see if we can make that happen without anyone even seeing us. If we get this right, we could be on our way back to your home without them realizing that Quinn's gone."

"All right." I could see that Heinrich was talking sense, but it was frustrating to have to wait even longer before seeing Quinn again.

One way or another, tomorrow I was going to rescue him, no matter what Heinrich said.

Day 20

"Right," whispered Heinrich, as we watched the camp from our vantage point up on a hill. "There seems to be eight men, all of them heavily armed."

"Easy peasy!" I scoffed. "I could eat eight humans for breakfast."

Heinrich glared at me.

"Sorry," I said meekly. "I meant that I could eat them if I ate humans, which of course I don't."

Heinrich sniffed and turned his head to watch the camp again. "All right. So far, we haven't been able to figure out where they're keeping Quinn, but your nose says that he's definitely down there somewhere."

"He is," I nodded. "And my nose is never wrong. Have you thought about what we're going to do if we don't see him anywhere? We can't snatch him back if we don't know where he is."

"Hmmm." Heinrich pondered for a moment but before he could suggest anything, I saw something that made me go red with rage.

There was Quinn being dragged around the camp on a leash!

"Quinn!" I roared, rearing up on my hind legs before racing down the hill to attack, all thoughts of our plan completely banished.

"Ferdinand! Wait! Come back!" called Heinrich, but I didn't care. I was going to get my boy.

I was blind to anything but my cub, batting humans out of the way as I headed straight towards him. If they hit me with their swords, I didn't notice, adrenaline coursing through my veins making me oblivious to the pain.

The human who was holding the end of his leash turned pale when he saw me running at him, teeth bared as I snarled a warning.

"That's right," I growled. "You let my son go! Come on, Quinn. We're getting out of here."

"But dad," protested Quinn.

"But dad, nothing," I snapped, snatching up his leash. "We don't have time for this. Let's go before the humans rally and come after us."

I ran back up the hill to where Heinrich was waiting, throwing splash potions at the humans who tried to follow us until they gave up and turned back to their camp.

At last, I judged that we were a safe enough distance away from the humans to stop running and I let go of Quinn.

"Quinn. My cub. I've missed you so much."

I leaned forward to hug him, but Quinn backed away.

"Why did you have to do that dad?" he wailed. "You've spoiled everything!"

Day 21

"Let me get this straight," I echoed. "You went with the humans out of choice?"

"That's right," nodded Quinn, huddling up next to the fire that Heinrich had built. I knew that going to gather firewood was his excuse to give us some time alone together and given what Quinn had just told me, I was grateful for the privacy.

"But why would you have done a stupid thing like that? Everyone knows that humans are bad news."

"I thought it would be fun," Quinn shrugged. "Now you've ruined everything. Those guys were my friends and you attacked them. For all I know, you could have killed them."

"I didn't kill anyone," I said dismissively, although the truth was that I had no idea how badly I'd hurt the humans. I'd been too focused on getting to Quinn. "Anyway, how could you have worried your mother like that? She's been absolutely distraught."

"I'm sorry dad," sniffed Quinn, tears starting to form in the corners of his eyes as he realized the severity of what he'd done. "I would have asked your permission, honestly I would have, but I thought you would say no."

"I would have," I nodded.

"And that's the problem! You never let me have any fun. I just wanted to see the world. When I met the adventurers, they invited me to go along and I knew they weren't going to wait around while I convinced you and mom to let me leave. I thought that if I went with them, I'd have a bit of fun and then come back once I'd had enough of exploring."

"But what was that business with the leash? You don't put a leash on someone who's your friend."

"Oh that. That was just for my protection. We'd met some other humans the day before and they looked like they were going to actually kidnap me for real so Cliff put the leash on me so that we could pretend that I was his pet and they'd leave me alone. They wouldn't have been able to get me away from him. Cliff is a really good fighter."

I stopped myself saying that he wasn't that good a fighter if I'd been able to get Quinn away from him.

"I'm sorry that I spoiled your fun," I said at last. "But you shouldn't have run away like that. We need to get you home so that your mom knows you're OK."

"All right," agreed Quinn, but he didn't seem excited at the thought.

Day 22

"Come on, Quinn. Pick your paws up! We've still got a long way to go before we get home," I called over my shoulder at my son.

"Yes, dad," he replied, but, if anything, he seemed to be walking even slower than before.

"Quinn…" I growled a warning, but Heinrich put out a hand to stop me going back to hurry him along.

"Give him a break," he advised. "I think he really liked the humans you took him away from. He didn't even get a chance to say goodbye to them. I'm sure he missed you and his mom, but it will be just as hard for him to leave his friends behind."

I looked back at my downcast son. Heinrich was right. He was not a happy cub.

I made a decision.

"All right, Quinn. How about if we go back to your friends so you can let them know that you're safe and with your family?"

"Can we?" His little face brightened up immediately and I knew it was the right thing to do.

"Just as long as we don't spend too long at their camp. Every minute we're away from home is a minute your mom has to wait for news."

"It won't be long at all, dad," Quinn promised. "I'll just say goodbye to everyone and then we can go home."

Day 23

I felt a twinge of shame when we reached the camp and I saw what a mess I'd made. Humans limped around, some with their arm in a sling, as they tried to repair the damage I'd done.

If only Quinn had told me where he was going, all of this could have been avoided. There was nothing left to do now but to go and apologize to them and hope that they wouldn't take revenge.

"Billy!" cried Quinn joyfully, running forward and jumping up at one of the humans, licking his face to say hello.

"Hi, Quinn. We weren't expecting to see you back," he remarked, patting Quinn on the head. When he saw me approaching behind him, however, he pulled out his sword. "Back off, bear!"

"I've come to say sorry." I held up my paws in a gesture of surrender. "I didn't mean to cause all this mess. I just wanted to rescue my cub. I didn't know that he'd gone with you willingly."

"What's this, Quinn?" Billy looked at the cub, frowning. "I thought you said it would be all right with your parents?"

Quinn blushed. "I'm sorry, Billy," he whispered. "I just wanted to have an adventure so I lied to you so that you would take me with you. I didn't realize that my dad would come after me."

"Of course he was going to come after you," exclaimed Billy. "He's your dad! It looks like you've got yourself into a fine mess, little bear."

"It sounds like you could do with a few extra paws to help tidy up," I offered.

"That would be great," smiled Billy.

We spent the afternoon helping repair the camp and by the time the sun set, everything was back the way it should be.

"Why don't you stay with us for dinner?" offered Billy.

"Can we dad? Can we?" pleaded Quinn and even Heinrich looked hopeful at the thought of a meal where he didn't have to cook for himself.

"All right," I finally agreed. "But we need to leave first thing in the morning. Your poor mom must be beside herself by now."

Quinn had the humans well trained and they placed an enormous plate filled with raw fish in front of me while they munched on pies and soups.

"These are very good fish," I complimented Billy. "Very good. It's almost as though a polar bear caught them."

"A polar bear did," he grinned. "You've got Quinn to thank for your dinner."

"Really?" I raised an eyebrow and looked at my cub, who blushed. "In that case, you'll have to come with me on the next fishing expedition. The pack could do with another fisherbear as talented as you."

"Thanks, dad," beamed Quinn.

"And you must all come back to our home and enjoy a polar bear feast," I said to the humans. "It's the least I can do to thank you for taking such good care of my son."

"A polar bear feast? I've never heard of such a thing," replied Billy. "That sounds like a lot of fun. We'd love to. Just give us a few days to join you. We've still got a bit of business to finish around here and we'll be there."

"You can't miss our home," I told him. "Just head out to the heart of the ice plains and go west at the lake. It won't be long before you're surrounded by polar bears and they'll escort you to the feast."

"Can't wait!"

Day 24

We got up bright and early in preparation for our long journey. It was a pleasant change to be going back in the direction of home instead of out into the unknown and a sudden impulse made me change route when we were faced with a choice of two paths.

"Where are we going, dad?" asked Quinn in surprise.

"You'll see," I replied mysteriously. "I've got something I want to show you and Heinrich."

The path started to head uphill, growing steeper and steeper as we made our way into the mountains. At last, we reached the pinnacle, the ice plains spread out before us.

"Wow," breathed Quinn, as Heinrich stood there speechless. "This is amazing!"

"This is home," I corrected. "All this is the realm of the polar bear."

Off in the distance, I was sure I could see the outlines of our polar bear family hunting and playing. It wouldn't be long before we were back with them, reunited as a family once more. But for now, we had enough time to take a moment and enjoy the view. If Quinn wanted to see the world, he couldn't do better than this.

Day 25

As we meandered through the mountains, Quinn chattered excitedly.

"Billy told me about all these cool places they were going to go. The reason why they couldn't come with us right away is because they're heading down into the mines to gather some resources to trade. They were then going to go to a village in the savannah. He said they wanted to get some sunshine and warmth after shivering in the ice plains."

Warmth? The ice plains were wonderfully warm! I had no idea what the human could have been talking about.

"The savannah sounds really interesting," Quinn continued. "Apparently horses run wild there. I'd love to see a horse in real life. Then they were going to go into the swamp."

Heinrich and I exchanged a look. "Witches live in swamps, you know," I told him.

"I know," Quinn replied. "Billy told me all about them. He and his friends are experts at fighting witches. They have a technique where some of them distract her while the rest of the gang sneak into her hut and clear out the potions. They then use her own potions against her to escape. It sounds like so much fun!"

As my son chattered on excitedly, I realized that there was no way that he was going to be content to stay in the ice plains with me and Rose. My boy was born for adventure and by the sounds of it, he'd picked the right people to protect him.

I was going to have to let him go one day or he was going to leave anyway. I just wasn't ready to say goodbye and deal with the uncertainty of never knowing when he was going to come back.

"Oh wow! Look at this!"

I was distracted from my thoughts by Quinn's shout. Heinrich and I hurried after him and found him swimming around in a pool.

"How cool is this? A secret pool hidden away in the mountaintop!"

I threw myself in the water after him and after a moment's hesitation, Heinrich joined us.

"Brrrr!" he shivered. "You could have warned me that the water was freezing!"

"What do you mean?" I laughed. "It's just right!"

Heinrich climbed out to go and build a fire to warm himself up while Quinn and I splashed about.

He might be planning on leaving home soon, but for now, I was going to enjoy the moment.

Day 26

THUNK!

I was woken by the sound of an arrow burying itself deep in the dirt inches away from my head.

"Skeleton attack!" yelled Heinrich, pulling out his sword as I jumped to my feet, but before I could launch myself at the skeleton, a bundle of white fluff shot past me and threw itself at the skeleton.

I watched in amazement as Quinn tore into the skeleton, the monster barely able to defend itself against the flurry of his attack. At last, I pulled myself together to join him and between the two of us, we quickly destroyed the creature.

"Well done, son," I told him, patting him on the back to congratulate him.

"Thanks, dad," he replied. "Billy has been teaching me some tricks. He said it was important to know how to defend yourself against anything so that you never had to be afraid."

"Wise words," I nodded. I couldn't be more proud. I knew that Quinn would grow up to be a powerful beast. All polar bear are. But I had no idea that he'd be quite so strong. His time with the humans had changed him in so many ways. My son seemed to have grown up during his weeks with them and I couldn't have wished for a better bear.

"Thanks for defending me," said Heinrich, breaking into my reverie. "I know that it's my fault the skeleton attacked. They would have left you alone if you didn't have a human with you. Perhaps it's time I went my own way now that you've got Quinn back."

"Don't be silly," I told him. "You're our friend and I want you to come to the feast too. It wouldn't be the same without you."

"Well in that case, I'd be delighted to join you," beamed Heinrich. "Maybe I can teach the other bears some human recipes and you could show me how to prepare fish polar bear style."

"That sounds like a great idea!" I smiled.

Day 27

"QUINN!"

Rose's scream of joy echoed through the plains when she saw her cub running towards her. You could have heard her all the way out in the savannah, she was so loud.

She raced towards Quinn who, for all his talk about wanting to grow up and see the world, had clearly desperately missed his mom.

The pair of them met and Rose squished Quinn into a huge bear hug, showering his snout with kisses.

"Aw, mom!" protested the cub, squirming in her arms, but it was clear that he didn't really mind.

"I am never, never letting you go," swore Rose as she rocked her little boy, still holding her in his arms.

"What if I need to go to the bathroom?" he asked.

"All right, son," I laughed, coming up behind them. "That's enough of your cheek. You know exactly what your mom meant."

"Thank you so much for bringing him back." Rose turned to me and threw herself into my arms, weeping with joy. "I was beginning to think I'd never seen either of you again."

"I'm sorry it's taken me so long to come back," I told her. "It's certainly been an adventure. Speaking of which, there's someone I'd like you to meet."

I beckoned to Heinrich and he came forward.

"This is Heinrich," I told her as he bowed to Rose.

"I'm delighted to meet you," he said.

"And you," replied Rose.

"Heinrich helped me find Quinn," I explained. "He helped me deal with the humans and without his map, I may never have found Quinn again."

"Ah yes. The humans who snatched our boy." Rose's face darkened.

"About that…" I coughed and shuffled my feet about. "It turns out that Quinn wasn't cubnapped at all. He went with the humans willingly. It seems that he wanted to have some adventure."

"Quinn!" gasped Rose, turning to look at her son. "How could you?"

"Sorry, mom." Quinn hung his head in shame.

"Don't be too hard on the lad," I advised. "But to make up for the fact that I destroyed the humans' camp to rescue him, I've invited them back here for a polar bear feast."

"A feast!" exclaimed Rose. "What a wonderful idea! Yes, we must have a feast to celebrate Quinn's return. I'll start preparing the food immediately."

"I'll take Quinn and Heinrich fishing," I said. "You can never have enough fish, after all!"

Day 28

I decided to take Quinn and Heinrich to the nearby creek instead of to the distant lake. The fish weren't as big there, but that way, Rose could keep an eye on him and see that he was fine after his adventure.

"Would you like me to show you how humans fish?" offered Heinrich.

I nodded and he pulled out a stick and some string from his bag. He tied them together and then threw the string into the water.

A few minutes later, he pulled it out and there, on the end of the line, was a hunk of rotten meat.

"Not to worry," I laughed at Heinrich's crestfallen face. "I'll show you how polar bears do it. We'll have plenty of fish by the time I'm finished."

I studied the water and a few moments' later, I scooped out a juicy fish.

"Your turn, Quinn," I said.

Quinn came up to the riverbank and watched the water, looking for signs of approaching fish. At last, he put a paw in the water and pulled out another fish.

"Is that how polar bears do it?" asked Heinrich. "That looks so much easier than using a fishing rod!"

"You said it," I grinned, as Heinrich lay on his belly so that his head overlooked the water. He examined the movements in the river and finally reached in to grab a fish…

…only to come up empty handed!

"It's impossible." He shook his head. "How are you supposed to get any fish like that?"

"You have to compensate for the way the light reflects in the water, like this." I showed him what I meant, demonstrating how the water made things look as though they were in a slightly different place and how to calculate to compensate for the difference. I pulled out fish after fish, never missing my target.

"Let me have another turn," said Heinrich at last. It took a few tries, but at last he finally managed to pull out a fish of his very own. It was only a small fry, barely a mouthful, but from the look of pride on his face, you'd have thought it was a giant shark.

That afternoon fishing with my friend and my cub was one of the best days of my life.

Day 29

"Billy's here! Billy's here!"

Quinn's excited shout announced the arrival of the human adventurers. Rose and I followed him out to where Quinn's friends were approaching. It felt strange to see Quinn so happy to see people, but it was clear from the way they behaved around each other that they'd become good friends in the time they'd spent together and he'd been well looked after.

"Billy!" I greeted as the human came towards me. "It's good to see you again."

"And you," nodded Billy. "Your home is lovely. We can't wait for the feast to start. Mining makes you really hungry!"

The humans were escorted to the feast area by a group of polar bears where they were given pride of place at the head of the clearing. Thanks to Heinrich, we were able to place bowls of cooked food in front of them, perfectly prepared instead of being burned to a crisp. I had to admit that even though Heinrich couldn't fish like a polar bear, he certainly knew how to cook like a human and judging by the expressions on Quinn's friends' faces, they were enjoying every mouthful.

When I'd given them enough time to eat their fill, I stood up, gesturing for quiet.

"I'd like to say a few words," I announced. "As you all know, my son Quinn went missing recently, assumed cubnapped. I went to rescue him, as any father would, and along the way I met Heinrich here, who became my friend. He helped me track down the humans Quinn was staying with, where I discovered that not all Minecraftians are evil cubnappers. Instead, it turned out that Quinn had made himself some friends, good friends who took care of him and protected him from danger so that he could see the world a little. I would like to take a moment to thank both Heinrich and the human adventurers for their kindness and for teaching me that not all human beings are evil." I raised my snout to the sky, roaring.

"To Heinrich and the adventurers!"

"To Heinrich and the adventurers!" echoed the rest of the polar bears, their growls and snarls creating a deafening cacophony.

Billy stood up. "I would like to thank *you*," he said. "Not just for such a magnificent feast but also for raising a wonderful young cub like Quinn. It was an absolute pleasure having him join us and he'd be very welcome to come along with us again if he ever wanted another adventure one day – as long as he asks his mom first this time!"

Quinn blushed as the rest of us laughed.

"Don't worry. I'm never going anywhere without checking with mom and dad first," he promised.

Day 30

All the polar bears gathered together to say goodbye to the humans, who were leaving for another adventure. Heinrich was leaving with them.

"I'd love to stay here with you," he'd told me last night, "but ultimately, I'm a human, not a polar bear, and it's a little too cold for me to live here. I'll be back to visit though, just you wait and see."

"Bye, Billy," sniffed Quinn as his friend leaned over to give him a hug. "Come back and see me soon?"

"Of course, little one," smiled Billy, ruffling the fur on Quinn's head affectionately before picking up his backpack and turning to me.

"Thank you again for your hospitality," he said. "Nobody knows how to put on a feast like a polar bear. Maybe one day you'll let Quinn come to our home town so we can return the favor."

"About that…" I looked at Rose and she nodded, giving me the go ahead to do what we'd discussed earlier. "Quinn, how would you feel about leaving with the humans?"

"Are you kidding?" Quinn's face lit up in delight. "I would LOVE that!"

"Only if it's OK with Billy and his friends," I cautioned.

"Of course it is," smiled Billy. "He's always welcome. You know that."

"Let me go grab my stuff and I'll be right with you."

Quinn rushed off to get a few things while Rose turned to me. "Are you sure we're doing the right thing in letting him go like this?" she asked. "He just seems so little."

"I know." I pulled her close to me. "He'll always be your baby cub. But like I told you, when I was his age, I left the ice plains for adventure. I'll never forget the good times I had on the road, but it gave me a newfound appreciation for the ice plains and now I'll never leave my home because I know that there's nowhere better. Quinn will come back feeling the same way too, you just wait and see."

At last, Quinn returned, his favorite teddy bear clutched tightly in his paws.

"All right mom, dad," he said. "I'm ready to go now. But don't worry. I'll send you a postcard very soon so you know everything that we do."

We gave him one final hug goodbye and then our cub and his human friends turned to leave.

"Make sure you always wash behind your ears!" Rose called after him.

"I will, mom!"

"And don't get into any mischief!" I yelled.

"I'll be fine…"

Something told me that, whatever happened, he really would be fine.